In Memory of ⸳

Who was born in the twentieth cent⸺ ⸺⸺ ⸺ the
twenty-first. In the course of his life he never smoked or
drunk nor did he ever wear trousers. He had no birth
sign.

Selling myself

I should explain from the outset that I need little exercise and I don't much like running. Running is fine if you're late for a bus or happen to be a whippet, but the concept of running in a circle for nothing but glory seems a bit medieval if you ask me. Along with this, I am not sleek. In fact, and to be brutally honest, I have the aerodynamic properties of a tortoise and the co-ordination of a potato salad. I did, however, put a lot of effort into running in my days at the greyhound track; my four legs would flail around like the Flying Scotsman's pistons. Despite this, you would need a Theodolite to establish whether I was actually moving forward. How can I put this? I'm not very fast. In fact, I am very slow. Slower than a dog with no legs. I was a bit of a duffer at the races. Unluckily for me I was born with a body that renders me quite incapable of doing anything very well.

Take me to the end of the road, and even with my homing gene, you and your children will be six feet under before I'm back.

I'll eat anything including holistic food and I only require a genteel daily walk. I am completely useless at retrieving sticks but I do love anyone that tickles my tummy. If a burglar did that, I'd love him just as much and even more if he gave me a ham sandwich. I'm a bit windy but not enough to increase global warming and kill polar bears. I don't whine when left alone and I don't need expensive bottled water. In the summer I laze about in the garden and in the winter I sleep so soundly you can use me as a draught excluder and I actually know more commands than I respond to.

I do not require a professional shampoo and blow-dry after every rain shower and unlike other dogs I am not kept alive with nothing but cash.

I don't do tricks. By which I mean I am *really* not able to do tricks, much as I am unable to fly through the air by flapping my arms (if indeed I have arms). It is not a question of me doing tricks badly but a question of me not being able to do tricks *at all*. Some cocky, wrong-headed fools skip about the place proclaiming, 'Why, that's nonsense! All dogs can do tricks, they just need training'. When I'm on my own, I *think* I can do tricks, but there is no way of testing it. If I imagine for a second that there is anyone in the house or in the garden, I freeze up. I think it must be a mental block.

I can't bowl, bat or catch, ski or dive and nor can I dance.

However, I am house-trained and never complain. If you feed me bread and cabbage for a week and turn off the central heating to save a bit of cash I will tell you cheerfully that things were much worse during my racing days. I am much kinder to the environment and your wallet than a personal trainer and I can be taken to any weekend gathering or dinner party without letting the side down.

Unless you are blind, a shepherd, a security guard or a policeman, dogs do not have a particular function, they are there to be loved, tickled and patted and to bring joy.

Sadly for most people though, looks are important and more so when choosing a dog so I don't get chosen, which is blushingly awful to admit. When I walk by people I don't attract lustful looks of desire or even faint glances of interest.

I suppose it is all part of me feeling as I did, and was in my racing days, a complete outsider. Wanting to be liked is often a very unlikeable characteristic and wanting to be hugged instead of beaten with a strap when I lost yet another race didn't win me any favours with my trainer.

In the fullness of time, I have no doubt that the ill treatment of all animals will be honed and chiselled to a point where the problems are gone. But time is one thing some of us animals don't have.

I'm going to have to break off now before I get all teary and stupid.

My Vision

Despite the best efforts of government ministers to build houses on every greyhound track in the south east of England, the rest of the country is still littered with them; Greyhound racing is a bit like breakfast telly - whether you like it or not, it exists. Which leads me nicely to my vision: to have an 'en vogue' football legend promote me in a dog magazine, introduce a celebrity culture of 'Big is Beautiful' and make us greyhounds as trendy as wine bars and social network sites, with some trendy disc jockey making an album called *Chill out Greyhound Session* which, according to the blurb on the cover, would be a laid-back mix of blissful greyhound noises sure to become the perfect soundtrack for your sushi and champagne dinner party. Greyhounds would become the most globally cooling dogs of all time, sharing a social plinth with that hairdresser from Reading who is famous for admitting a fondness for blinking. We would celebrate the sponsorship nationally with the most important part of any ceremony - fireworks. Sadly, this is where my vision falls down. Fireworks make me shake uncontrollably and pee my bed. Perhaps the money from the sponsorship should be spent instead on combating disease and buying saveloys? And if it all went wrong I would blame the government.

In short our government isn't interested in saving lives, (certainly not greyhounds'); it's only interest is in raising money from taxation and forcing supermarkets to put 'best before' dates on everything. We have a civil service that is busy posting out notices to give us advice about recycling but then when we've finished reading the leaflet we have to decide whether it goes in the blue bin or the black one as it has a slight plastic lamination, so is it paper or plastic?

We are ostracized for putting our refuse in the wrong colour bin and the only way we can get a dopamine rush is by taking the dog for a walk.

This is where I come in. What is needed to get round this whole problem is to adopt a greyhound, who will happily eat your leftovers, freeing up your green bin for leftover chocolate, which in recorded history nobody has ever thrown away.

If I'd been born to a wealthy, intelligent family; I could have gone to obedience classes in Chelsea, (although I've heard these schools are tough especially the homework), I'd have gained brilliant doggy social skills with almost no effort at all, lived in the comfort of a hedge fund as opposed to a hedgerow, been well fed and owned a diamond studded collar. Some dogs win the lottery. And some don't. If you are born a greyhound with black fur and are rubbish at running, things are likely to be a little more difficult. Every year hundreds of us hounds have to overcome the massive problem of being made to run like there's red hot chilli up our rear end, because we're just not cute enough or small enough to make it into some lady's pink handbag or into the family photograph album. Any dog that slows down or is unprofitable is killed. I've said before that to be born a Chihuahua and cute is to win the first prize in the lottery of life; to be a short haired black dog the height of a normal person's navel is more like the booby prize.

Trust me; greyhound racing is controlled by gambling and money. The majority of people attending these races have little knowledge of what actually happens to us. Little do they know and little do they care. It is big business with total disregard for us dogs.

The life of a racing greyhound is one of misery, fear, mistreatment and finally a painful death.

The inhuman treatment of us greyhounds is beyond comprehension. Mostly, our horrible short life begins the day we are born and ends the day we die.

Despite the terrible lives which many racing greyhounds are forced to endure they generally adapt well to life after racing. In some instances however, some dogs do bear the scars of their life. I know I do. Sometimes when I encounter a pyramid of baked beans I am tempted to push it over. Don't you?

What I'm trying to say is that owning a greyhound should be like owning a Lamborghini, tell someone at a dinner party you have one and in minutes you will be the most popular person there. Someone should stop the indiscriminate breeding of greyhounds for racing purposes. My reason? Well, why don't you join me on my descent into the waking nightmare of homelessness?

Rant over.

Homelessness

During the summer of 2011 I ended up living in a box in Canterbury. Before this, the only homeless dogs I had ever seen were tied to rather frightening-looking, foul-mouthed men who prowled the streets begging for money. I used to belittle homeless people. I would stupidly blame them for adding to their burden by buying a dog and I was convinced that Big Issue sellers would sell a lot more copies if they smartened themselves up a bit, instead of looking like tramps. How ignorant I was and how very scary it is to find oneself with no friends, no family and nowhere to stay. I often think about how terrible that moment was when I realised, for the first time, that I had no bed for the night; slipping into a cold doorway and being serenaded to sleep by a passing drunk, knowing that the price to pay for a few cold chips is a half-hour, meth soaked lecture on God's infinite wisdom from your new companion.

One such man was a good master for a while, keeping the wolf from the door but nothing much else. When drunk, which he was often, he would shout at me if I stretched out looking for an extra 2mm of legroom. I would respond without fuss or murmur as in this paralytic state he would soon fall asleep with that stupid smile people have when their arteries are full of cheap cider.

Some people do give you pitying looks and one even brought me supermarket ham which was bright pink and about as nutritional as the plastic bag it came in. Mostly, though, I was subjected to much derision, people would point and laugh or raise their eyebrows and edge away.

The memory sends a shiver down my spine even now.

Then there is the hen party. Overwhelmingly rude groups of women with bright orange complexions and special-forces tattoos that conga out of the pubs at two in the morning. Hen parties have bestridden the most beautiful of towns for a quarter of a century, sowing discord, agitation and dismay. Their power grows daily and their disciples are many. The signature dish of these anti-social revellers is the kebab and after many hours of binge-drinking they stop to squat and pee in shop doorways. Unable to master the etiquette of shoving the kebab between the immense, wobbly mounds of flesh on their chests whilst doing the necessary, they put the kebab on the floor beside them. That is my happiest moment.

I have some advice for any dog whose life has gone so far down the toilet that he's only reading a newspaper because he's sleeping on it. If you hole up for a night in a shop doorway in the town, those street-cleaner men will come along and squirt you with powerful jets of icy water. And then, when you're soggy and cold, you'll be moved to another doorway where a drunken late-night reveller will be sick all over you. And to make matters worse you'll spend your days scouring the city streets for out-of-date sandwiches, while stinking. All the while you'll be surrounded by people who are popping out to shop because there's no more room in their house for any more designer dogs. Such dogs are cherished members of the family, they are status symbols, they are art, they are glamorous, they are cool. My God, I want a home so badly that it hurts.

When you have a loving owner and a full stomach, Canterbury is truly one of the best places on earth.

But when you have nothing, it is more depressing than listening to a pop star wannabe struggling through 'Hallelujah' on a pub karaoke night. So I made a decision to leave my cardboard home in Canterbury where the only knowledge I gained whilst there was that recently defunct and apparently worthless European coins still work as legal tender for buskers and beggars and that alcohol makes an ideal substitute for happiness.

What I want to say about all this is that I don't expect your pity or understanding (although I wouldn't throw either out of bed), but perhaps the sense of fear of eternal unhappiness, the insecurity, the misery, that I felt are prey to us all? I do hope so. I would feel the most conspicuous oddity otherwise.

Wearing my mask of a placid, failure of a greyhound which had become so tight it had re-designed whatever true face once screamed behind it, I decided to take a stroll to the countryside, where food simply wouldn't be an issue - or so I thought. I left Canterbury with just the fur I had on me and a half-eaten Mars bar. I would find stuff along the way, making it more of an adventure, I assured myself. But after two days of walking through stubble fields where the vicious little stalks removed several hairs and a great deal of skin from my feet, I felt I may have made a bad decision. To compound my misery, there were no tasty snack bars here either.

I look back and I wonder what on earth was going on in my head when I chose to live in the countryside rather than the town. But then I consoled myself by thinking of those in power who can't make a sensible decision either.

The countryside for me is a strange and frightening place full of limitless possibilities for ending up dead in a ditch. I would have sat down at the side of the road and wept solidly but for an overwhelming fear of something like a bear coming along and eating me.

A tip here, if you do end up in the countryside, avoid any small dead brown animal that looks like a lamb chop because it's disgusting and it's certainly not a lamb chop. I did find several thousand potatoes in one field and, outside someone's kitchen window, a half-eaten pork pie. There were even some cows for company but they made an enormous song and dance every time I walked past. I know it sounds like a hideous way to live until you remember that when the sun sinks you don't have to hole up under some railway bridge.

There are countless stables full of straw where you can keep warm in fertiliser bags and it's still possible to find a barn that hasn't been converted into an agreeable home by someone called Hugo. It might even turn out to be fun, I first thought. Not as much fun as being the Queen, but certainly not bad. I could laze around and catch rabbits and dig dens and it'd be like being a pup again. Or I could be mistaken for a mutant squirrel and shot by someone wearing camouflage trousers and left to rot in the woods where passing ramblers would complain of the smell.

Come to think of it, initially I was surprised that the countryside wasn't awash with tramps and their dogs, as in the time I lived there, I didn't see even one. There was a man, with a spaniel on a piece of rope, selling the Big Issue outside the village Post Office, but I frequently saw them both in a BMW and sleeping in that doesn't count.

I did pass a farm shop once. Actually, it wasn't really a farm shop at all, because the floor was covered in expensive rugs rather than fertiliser bags and all the staff looked like supermodels instead of pickled walnuts.

Inside you could buy cellophane packs of what can only be described as bird seed and jumpers made from exotic animals that resembled that pushmi-pullyu thing from *Doctor Dolittle* and bread that cost fifty pounds. Everything in the shop was sold with that all-important eco tag. This all sent the surrounding house prices rocketing upwards. People would pay considerably more to live in this village because the price of the cheese is the same as that of a small car.

Finally one of the pretty young sales girls came outside so I asked her if there was any tasty morsel that might qualify as food going begging. She looked perplexed. Is there anything in there that once had a face? Or anything that resembles a custard cream? Bewildered, she walked away and came back with a bowl of lettuce. 'No,' I said, 'I am not a rabbit. I am a fully grown racing greyhound. I am hungry and I want a bargain bucket family feast. After five minutes of her looking vacant, I decided the tastiest things in the shop must be the tables and chairs so I bid her farewell.

I'd started to look like a piece of black string with a knot in it. The rumbling of my once immense stomach and the rattling in my chest was startling all sorts of animals that would have remained hidden and unseen to the tiptoeing rambler.

Present a wild animal with a bearded biped in a cagoule and the animal would remain *in situ,* holding its breath until the fool had gone away. Present it with a dog and it'll leap out of its burrow, or nest or sett. Deer shot out of every bush, badgers scampered out of their holes and with blinking eyes, rushed off to alert their mates. Rabbits snouted and foxes looked on slyly, wondering if they could beat me in a fight and then eat me.

A bark from me even managed to scare a family of barn owls, and normally you'd need a night-vision lens, a night without sleep and several months in hospital recovering from hypothermia to see one of those. I love barn owls and seeing some during the day was sensational.

Then I spotted what appeared to be a hare leaping about. Over my racing years there have been a great many hares and none of them, if I'm honest, have been any good or even realistic. Oh, there might have been some fast ones and some with great charisma. Mostly, they have been pretty as well.

But to eat? No, they were the dog track equivalent of a polystyrene cup. Cheap, plastic and at the right time, and in the right place, sort of fun to play with. But not today, I couldn't be bothered and I was tired.

It was to be one of the longest and most miserable nights of my life. The hunger in my belly is so vibrant that it has become an all-consuming entity. Sleep is impossible. All I can think about is food. As night fell I was too exhausted and broken to move. In fact, after a few hours I began to think that Dante had got everything wrong. There are not nine circles of hell. There are ten.

There would then follow a screech of brakes, tyre squeal and headlights which sent me hurtling into a bush where a half-eaten pizza thrown from the car window hit me full on in the face followed shortly after by the box it had been delivered in. I now know that even in my new found poverty, I could still be happy.

An approaching thunderstorm growled menacingly overhead.

Rescue

Back to my story and the next day along came my saviour in an old woody, leathery chariot called a Wolseley which was the automobile equivalent of the tweed jacket and plaid skirt in which she dressed. A slightly plump woman called Flavia, who wore sun glasses when it wasn't sunny, bedecked with a charity 'Deed not Breed' T-shirt hastily pulled down over her normal clothes and a steely resolve to rescue me from my nomadic existence by offering me a lift to a local centre for re-homing dogs.

It was late, dark, cold and pouring down. I was soaking wet and by this time the rain was ruining my hair, I was hungry. I wanted a cauliflower. I wanted a chicken leg, cold with some mayonnaise. I would have torn out my own eyes for a blood-red fillet steak. This all meant I was faced with a choice: get in the car and hope the woman isn't a murderer whose aim is to make me into a pasty and serve me up at the next W.I. meeting or stay where I was and spend the rest of my life being hungry and possibly ending up in a pasty anyway.

The interior of the car smelt of Bakelite headlights and wartime ration books not that I knew that precise smell.

'Figgy oatcake?' she asked.' They're awfully healthy.'

I could gripe a bit if I wanted to. The re-homing centre did need a lick of paint and the doors needed oiling but on the plus side it had patio heaters, which got my vote and all day T.V. albeit broadcast mute, and with sub-titles in what I supposed was Latin.

The kennels were much more comfortable and quiet than I expected. My kennel was devoid of any kind of frivolity. It was a three-star sort of place and the sleeping area was a bit small and I banged my head every single time I climbed inside, but I could live with that.

Potential owners came and went. They tried to be kind, saying that I was very black and unusual. But the simple fact of the matter is that I'm ugly and black because this is the colour of my heart. I would ask them politely to leave me alone. I even turned my back on them to show disinterest. If asked, I would have told you that I was happy. I was content, which will have to do for most of us.

Then along came the three boys. Plainly, these boys' parents were useless - they probably had the parenting skills of a panda, allowing their boys to be out and about, harassing us dogs at will. After being jeered and spat at for the fourth time, I stood up to my full height, puffed out my chest and stared at the boys through the bars - by sheer luck the ringleader stopped his torrent of abuse and I explained firmly that it would be best if he went back to whichever stone he had crawled from. Translated into human speak, this came out as loud barking. At this precise moment the parents arrived back, reached for their mobile phones and began to take pictures of the altercation. That put me in a tricky spot. I'm a dog and I don't know how old a child is. The boy I was looking at through the bars could have been 28. Or he could have been 8. I figured the photographs could look a bit like me bullying him, and instead of worrying that I would be put down I was actually thinking 'Jeez, I'm going to get done for assault if I'm not careful'.

I stopped my noise and lay back down on my bed and, in a flurry of swearing and hand gestures involving fingers, they were gone. Leaving me with a serious problem. A poor quality photo of me with one mutilated ear, accompanied by a 'Sticky Dog' notice went up on the kennel's notice board. How had I not noticed that? Where was my other ear? I wasn't born like this; I had two ears at the greyhound track. Was this the reason why no mention was ever made of my racing history? It had all gone apart from one tattoo number, along with a large chunk of my left ear.

Sticky Dog

These days everyone has a camera phone which means I have my photograph taken about two million times a day. I hate it with an unbridled passion. The photograph serves as a permanent reminder that I am just a one-eared huge stomach with a large chin and a piece of wire wool growing out of it. I look horrible in pictures because I look horrible in the flesh.

Things got worse.

After a short walk the following day accompanied by the owner's wife Beryl, an eternal source of delight to me, I arrived back at my kennel to be greeted by a mysterious blonde lurcher wearing a ludicrous red spotted hanky round her neck.

She was a real heart-stopper, a piece of art who explained to me in broken English, that my room had been let to her as all the other kennels were fully booked. So we had to share.

My kennel mate's name had too many vowels in it to be pronounceable. It began with a V and then I had to make the sort of noise a cat would emit if its tail was trodden on. She'd also eaten my lunch. I wore a groove in the floor that day with endless trips to my dinner bowl, hoping against hope that I had somehow missed a cold sausage on the previous 4,000 excursions. I tried to sound happy about the situation, but there was a baleful look in my eyes that said it all. I feared that, before long, my room would be all Laura Ashley chintz and co-ordinated cushions.

V had an over-inflated sense of self-importance. She said she chose to stay in this particular rehoming-centre whenever she was in town because it's comfortable and convenient. She is absolutely convinced that she is in some way special, different, interesting and worth having round for dinner, which was true. I could clearly see that she stood out in the kennels much like a super model at a bus stop. Whilst I, on the other hand, just wanted to be seen as 'the same' as everyone else.

V said that at home in Russia she had a wardrobe of outfits that stretched from here to Peru so that she never turned up anywhere wearing the wrong clothes. 'I mean,' she said 'can you imagine going to Ascot in a silver space-suit? It would be social suicide.'

Unfortunately, my situation in the kennel was becoming increasingly fraught with difficulties. Yes there may be space in the sleeping quarters for two dogs but only if one dog had no legs. V was surprisingly well kitted out with toys which she insisted having with her at all times. This meant I spent half the evening backing up into a tiny space in which I could wait while Lady V with her lovely hair and mouthful of toys squeezed by.

I decided to sleep outside in the main kennel area on a pillow that had a huge hump in the middle and didn't absorb dribble. I did miss the sound of V breathing and the waft of warm air onto the back of my neck from her flatulent bottom, but not the crying and whimpering in her sleep.

Fortunately, I didn't have to share for long. The following week someone arrived in a flurry of excitement, making a huge fuss of my roommate. V collected her belongings - a small half eaten tennis ball, a headless doll in a pink tutu and a rubber biscuit - and set off into the world in the back of an old Volvo estate. I found out later that this was to be her third owner in as many years. V suffered from "separation anxiety" I overheard one kennel maid say. Once the new owners find out how noisy and destructive she is when left alone, she'll be back at the kennels again'.

I was saddened by this revelation but at the same time deeply, properly, neck-reddening jealous. Dammit - I never barked, why didn't anyone want me?

Simply there is no call for an ugly dog like me. I could only be part-exchanged with some used bus ticket.

Plainly I was hurt by this thought and wanted someone to hug some sympathy into me. I desperately wanted someone to adopt me; it was more pressing than my next breath.

Adoption

Luckily for me the kennel owner operated a strict 'no competition' rule when we were out in the paddocks playing. They started the games, ball throwing mostly, and we dogs exerted energy and then the games finished. There were never any winners and consequently there were never any losers. The no competition ruling also applied to the local village fête, which arrived in the summer along with the wisteria. There was, however, a competition for the biggest turnip, best pasta salads and scummiest quiche baking. But all of these paled alongside the dog show war. Which is why I got up at 4.30 am that day - to start preening myself in the hope that my bright, shiny black, patent-look coat would disguise the fact that I had one missing ear and grey whiskers sprouting from my several chins. Nobody was going to push me out of the limelight into the prize lupins. Nobody was going to make joke retching noises behind my back. I was out there to win, to crush the competition like beetles. I'd be in the midst of it all shouting 'Pick me, pick me'.

Flavia appeared in her yellow bagginess. 'Don't worry Jack,' she kept saying, 'do your best. It's not the winning.' She was so kind, she almost managed to shut down the nerves shaking in my hind legs.

'They are all lovely,' said the judge, sticking to the spirit of the day. What spirit? What's the point of protecting us dogs from the horror of failure at the dog show when the owners are all giving one another Chinese burns behind our backs? 'My dog's better than yours. Say it! Say it!'

I spoke to an English setter who said he came in second last year. His owner took the cup he won to the engravers and had it inscribed with a big '1st'.

After the judging Flavia appeared again to say 'Hello'. She didn't want me to see she was unhappy but it had broken her heart when, as predicted, I was last in the show. 'I have seen more attractive boils' said one woman, who had modelled her hair on Einstein. 'What on earth was its owner thinking of?' another asked.

We have all sat with brows furrowed feeling incredibly dumb as someone asks us to respond to an image or line of verse.

What do you think Keats was referring to here?

What does Robert Browning achieve by using his metaphor?

What was Picasso trying to portray here?

It brings it all back doesn't it? All the red-faced, blood-pounding humiliation and embarrassment of being singled out for comment. This is how I felt right now.

Flavia could tell that I was fighting back the tears. She said 'Cheer up Jack, there will be more shows in the future and you'll win next time around. Do you give up the Sunday kick-around because you'll never be Thierry Henry? Of course not. We don't stop talking about how the world might be a better place just because we have no chance of making it to Prime Minister. It really is enough in life to just have fun'. Wise words indeed Flavia, but I was a dog with no sense of politics or talent for football. Becoming an attractive dog to the human race isn't something I can learn from a 'How To' book and some crayons.

I cannot read and write or understand many spoken words. But I understand what you'd like me to do in other ways. Go left, go right, sit, and lie. And think how thrilled I am when you feed me and pet me and take me out for a walk. Now try to imagine how I would feel if you locked me up one night. And never came back. That is how I feel now.

I consoled myself with the fact that all the funniest dogs I'd ever met were abject, total failures and mostly ugly. But deep inside I want to be loved. I just want to matter.

This is why I felt a certain sense of pride as we trudged home from the village fête. Everyone else was carrying rosettes and cups but my heart was thrashing away in my ribcage as I walked away with Flavia and her winning smile.

And so, with a spring in my step and hope in my heart, I arrive at the door to Flavia's house.

"Slow-cooked lamb shanks for supper?" asked Flavia. The four horsemen of the Apocalypse couldn't have dragged me from that opportunity.

Flavia

After a few days I managed to have a snoop around Flavia's living quarters, which provided a rare insight into the life of the landed gentry. The house had dark Elizabethan beams and the sitting room walls were panelled in wood. Some of the panels were obviously doors in a previous life and there were areas of medieval painted plaster. There were bookshelves and windows with leaded panes of warped glass of great antiquity and far from contemptible furnishings. There was a Bang and Olufsen CD player and TV together with a symphony of gloomy portraits - unsmiling ancestors with splashes of pure ostentation and gilt. In the sitting room, blue and gold striped Rococo sofas clashed violently with the bright red heavily patterned carpet. In short, when I start to dribble and need lengthy veterinary care, Flavia's furniture could be sold to pay for it.

The heating was turned up too high and she cooked things I'd never seen before. I was as well set up as any dog could be so I just smiled the smile of a dog at peace with himself.

My dinner that first evening was full of things nestling on other things. Delicious! I was living in the home of someone who didn't have the IQ of a daffodil and the conversational ability of a cushion. I had Flavia, who laughed like a drain whenever I looked at her.

I spent halcyon days watching Flavia and her friends, clad largely in tweed and Viyella, making food out of tofu and lentils.

They would sit around knitting underwear out of hemp, taking time out to discuss the issues of the day like climate change, flower arranging and felting.

Their chatter and laughter fills the air. Flavia would make them laugh with oblique references to Dickens and the iniquities of the local planning office. She could recite, like many of her generation but with more perfect recall than most, all the usual nursery rhymes along with most of Lewis Carroll and other hardy annuals. I know all this is very mockable, very sensible cardigan-wearing reading-glasses on a thin gold chain stuff but it was such a solace to me in a world full of Twitter trolls, school bullies and grisly greyhound killings.

I would sit for hours with Flavia working on a crossword or reading a book. Sunday evenings were my favourite, amateur dramatics night at the local shabby without the 'chic' village hall. Big boxes of tea bags, which I have failed to acquire a taste for and packets of biscuits stand on a trestle table at one end of the room. I can still smell that rehearsal room and hear its piano. The play they were about to put on was a musical so the best casting I could ever hope for would be in a non-singing role as Mrs Higgins dog, in My Fair Lady which was an especial triumph. That was the sum total of my dramatic experience, nativity plays aside when I was the dog in a manger. Yet I had it in my head that I was a natural actor, that I knew how to speak lines and have a presence on stage.

I was so happy; you could have taken out my liver and fed it to the cat. And I wouldn't have noticed.

We had holidays together, mostly in France where she would cast aside her tweed and don her designer kaftan.

Flavia arranged for me to have a doggy passport so we could go to somewhere that has the best scenery in the world and is replete with funny-looking villagers who sit outside their houses in baggy clothing. But unlike people in other parts of the world, they don't pester you for money, or try to sell you paper napkins and hot dogs at traffic lights.

France is beautiful and the French language is spoken honey. They are also very good at cheese and wine.

One year we went to St. Tropez where I have never seen such expensive hair in all my life. The whole place was crammed with people and their accessorised dogs, so bewitchingly beautiful, that I felt like a zoo animal stood next to Flavia.

Mind you, if you set foot in any of the shops, you are made to feel about the height of a Pekinese or smaller, because it is immediately apparent that you cannot afford to buy a single thing they have on offer. It's all Prada and Armani. God knows where the locals buy a box of dog biscuits or a toilet roll.

Strangely, however, it was the most relaxing place I'd ever visited. Nobody is rushing about, people have time to stroll and chat in the street, or fit in a cocktail. Probably, this is because the jet set has no real concept of time. They don't have to be at meetings because they don't have jobs and if they have a plane to catch, it'll wait, as it's their own. I loved the south of France and found it fascinating. If I had a chance to come back as anyone, at any time in history, I would want to be here in the company of Flavia and Coco Chanel on some iconic speedboat of the 1960s with its Cadillac-like interior and airliner-inspired fold down drinks tray full of steak and kidney puddings.

Back home in the summer, there was the annual Flower Show which continued to be a huge attraction to the villagers and surrounding locals. This year, it even managed to attract me. However, the flowers bored me and I considered the astro turf on the tables to be there solely for me to pee on, which got me some fierce looks. Happily, the people who visited the show weren't boring at all. There were those people who liked gardens to be traditional and others who wanted a Technicolor riot of flora and fauna. These people are called gardeners. They would stand for hours eyeing up trowels and arguing about the finest topsoil and organic compost that money could buy.

There were tractors and beehives and people everywhere laden with toddlers in wellies and others trying to break the speed limit by riding a cow.

But the best thing about any village show is the burger van.

Someone famous was signing a book in a marquee and whilst we queued for a glass of wine in a plastic cup we got to see the celebrity for real propping up the bar in the beer tent. The whole event was smart and sponsored by local dignitaries.

People elsewhere were busy erecting bits of canvas to keep the wind off the home made vol-au-vents and quails egg soup. It was bliss, or it would have been if the chap on the public address system had shut up for one minute so that we could hear the brass band playing.

Then things started to go a bit pear-shaped. My first disappointment came when I looked down and noticed I was wearing what looked like a skeleton outfit. The second came when I discovered I'd been entered into a fund raising fancy dress fun run in aid of the local dogs re-homing centre. I had finally drawn the dog's equivalent of life's short straw. Flavia looked down at me, patted my head and smiled her reassuring smile. I would have been more relaxed if I'd had my toenails torn out while being force-fed wallpaper paste. And I was not alone. The pug and the miniature something or other standing next to the prize rhubarb, were dressed as pirates and were surrounded by two women - a little larger than normal, who were so angry about their dogs having identical outfits that after a bit of scuffle, withdrew them from the competition.

Unbelievable.

Most entrants in the dog fancy dress competition were hybrids with a poodle mix, making them designer dog experimentations costing more than a house and I'm afraid the subject of some bitter controversy in dogdom.

One such dog, a Cockerpoo called Gary, told me that in addition to his designer collar costing 900 quid he had a microchip inserted into his skin so he can be tracked by satellite, which cost his owner another million pounds. Dog ownership in Britain, he said, is dropping and more people owned a fish nowadays than owned a dog. Gary claimed that because of changing life-styles, children prefer virtual pets on their computers and parents don't want to leave a real dog at home all day in case it eats the laptop and pees on the organic carpet. Also when a dog dies, you can't flush it down the toilet.

Needless to say I didn't win the 'fun run', I'm not sure I even completed the race. As mentioned beforehand, I can run, but only as well as I can tie shoelaces, but the atmosphere on the day was very jolly and we did raise a lot of money. It was this day that I discovered I had the underdog sympathy gene. People reviewing my performance at running said I was brave and plucky and full of spirit. They would forgive me anything, even when I'd eaten a prize cake and topped off the day by being sick on the vicar's feet.

We went home that evening accompanied by a few of Flavia's friends and played cards. It was brilliant. The room was full of canapés, wine, trumps and tension. There was no television, no computer and no piano playing just the four of them sitting there, a bit drunk, in a room full of lies, with a fist full of rubbish.

Christmases, with its horrid jumpers and falling asleep in front of the Queen, came and went.

Bill

Pretty soon I was 7 years old and sleeping a lot. The sun had moved across the sky as though God's finger was on the fast forward button. Blink and you miss a whole year. The years had blended and blurred in my mind.

Then all hell broke loose. Flavia became ill. Her friend Bill - in a seemingly endless custody battle with his ex-wife, who had obviously been touched by the breeze of insanity - moved me into his ground floor flat to live with him and his teenage son. Bill thought the idea of 'going for a walk' completely ludicrous because only one thing will happen, you will end up back at home again. So what's the point of going out in the first place? The son's reasoning for not going out was similar. He said he didn't need to go outside as he could see all sorts of interesting things if he simply stayed indoors and watched them on his computer. He claimed that the air in the sitting room near the PlayStation was just as fresh as the air in the garden.

I alleviated the boredom of the flat by strolling out through the garden, which had obviously been created by an unimaginative designer with no interest in his brief. I stopped for a moment to admire one particular flower bed that was filled with crushed blue glass. It looked wonderful, a cheerful alternative to the dreary brownness of soil or grass. I was about to cock my leg for a pee when a man leapt out from nowhere. 'I wouldn't do that' he warned 'Unless you want to get your owner evicted'. I went to sleep that night a bit dejected. And my mood darkened during the following week. That's when it happened. Bill went on a business trip and left me with the son.

Boredom set in after two days. I started to chew the advertising inserts that came through the letterbox and fell on the floor. I paced up and down the hallway, breaking interior fixtures and fittings and generally killing everything in the garden with dog pee.

The son was a normal mono-syllabic, teenage chap who chose to wear his hat back to front, and his trousers in such a way that you could see his pants. He didn't interact with me or take me out for a walk. He made no effort to smile or chat but instead spent every waking hour sitting in front of a computer screen which had taken over his life along with texting. His only break from this pursuit was when he was talking into his mobile phone ordering pizza and forgetting to buy dog food. He was more insanely in love with this piece of technology than anything he had ever owned before. He had no need for human relationships when he had his computer.

I started listening to the voices in my head, telling me to get out. As I wandered around the flat for the millionth time desperate for a pee, I started to feel pangs of insecurity and somewhat like the baton in a relay race. So the following night when the son's friends shuffled in with their un-tucked shirts and their dreadful shoes, I crept out through the open door. I left them watching clips on YouTube of young men falling off motorcycles. They didn't even notice I had gone.

I missed Flavia. I missed her laughter and her cuddles. This was the reason I decided to move on and find my way back to the re-homing centre. How hard could it be?

Speaking with the benefit of experience and the gift of hindsight, I assure you that I should have stayed at Bill's place. But I was hungry and my stomach is more important to me than the Royal Wedding or the war in the Middle East.

The Garden of England

I must say at this juncture that I don't like fighting. I prefer passive resistance and, if that doesn't work, active fleeing. Once, at the greyhound track, I had a bit of play fight with one of the other dogs - we pranced around each other making snarly faces until he accidentally bit me on the leg and I simply could not believe how much it hurt. 'Ow,' I said in a rather un-canine way.

So you can imagine my consternation when I was stopped in my tracks by a large ginger tom, sunning himself on the pavement in front of me. He was bereft of anything except perhaps a sense of menace; a menace that would have made me want to put my wallet down the front of my underpants, had I had either. But I said to myself, this is okay. This is a rough area where you don't say 'Excuse me kind sir, please stand aside, I'm coming through'. So I broke into a brisk saunter and crossed the road, avoiding any eye contact with said feline.

With nothing but the sun for guidance I continued my journey through Kent, confident in the knowledge that I was a dog with a sense of direction and a basic grasp of English. After three hours I still hadn't passed any eateries with bins housing decent steak or smoked salmon waiting to be liberated. I think it's worth pausing here for a moment to say that, over the years, I have eaten a blackbird, several worms, indeterminable road kill and a discarded anchovy from a pizza at Bill's place. To continue, I'd arrived in Sandwich, one of the most affluent, sought-after areas in Kent - a four bedroom house in Sandwich costs more than a book of stamps - yet there was only one worthwhile restaurant with bins outside.

One eatery only and it was empty, so no leftovers. I was disappointed and, being a dog, unable to ask anyone for directions. In any case, if I could ask I can't listen. It is a known fact, and it has been since the dawn of time, that a dog will hear only his own name and then shut down.

I was now extremely hungry and I started to worry that, should I be found dead in the street I had no recognisable markings or identification. I'm just a black silhouette of a dog with one ear.

Having spent a whole day on what seemed like a mammoth tour of Kent without food, I thought about following the epic tale of Tony Bullimore, who started to eat himself after his yacht capsized in the ocean. Instead I lay down on some new turf which, due to the blistering heat of the day looked like sisal matting, and fell asleep. I woke abruptly some time later to the sound of a woman's voice: 'O-M-G, Rupert. Come here. There's a dog that looks like Van Gogh (pronounced Go)'. I was too distracted by the triple beef burger smothered in tangy, slightly sweet creamy sauce, topped with gherkin and cheese, slapped into a triple decking of sesame seed bunnage that she was holding in a Styrofoam tray to worry that she might be the ringleader of a Kentish based international dog fighting gang. I didn't even notice that I'd woken up in the garden of a substantial wisteria-softened house with a swimming pool.

'O-M-G' (again) 'He looks starving. Here Vincent, have the rest of my burger' she said. 'Vincent' was to become my new name hereafter. Being fed a Whopper burger at this point in my life was about as close to heaven as I could get while my heart was still beating.

I stretched out feeling a bit light headed then looked up and saw the girl's orangeness and her lips - so full of collagen she looked like a huge Satsuma.

'I'll phone the R.S.P.C.A. and get the dog picked up' said her co-finder brother Rupert who was 10 per cent designer stubble and 90 per cent teeth.

Now I don't normally have dealings with the RSPCA as I am a dog but that said it's hard to condone wanton cruelty and I was so gut gnawingly hungry that I was about to start eating my own leg, which is most definitely cruel.

Katie

I was taken into the house by her orangeness where I was introduced to a lovely chap, Colin a unique-looking hairless Chinese Crested, which I presumed was a dog. Colin claimed to have come second at Crufts in 2008. This was because, he explained, after he sat down on command he became distracted by another dog and stood up again. All year he had been preparing for his moment of glory and because of one pesky dog he had been beaten into second place by a yorkie. You had to be there to see the unbearable sadness in Colin's eyes as he told me his sorry tale.

Colin said he is typical of his breed. He is happy, animated and agile. He is an adept climber and jumper who often grips his toys (or his owner's neck) tightly with his paws. He was very "people-oriented" and demanded a lot of personal interaction from his owner but was a bit reserved with strangers, stand-offish in fact with new people. However, frequent socialization and behavioral training had helped him build his confidence. 'The advantage of being a naked dog like me is no body odour, no hair to shed and no fleas.'

Colin didn't bark much and when he did nobody could hear him, so he wouldn't make a good watch dog. Also, when taken out for a walk he needed sun block to help reduce sun burn and required a decent moisturiser rubbed in before bed time.

He said that a scientist at some University announced that if you eat two tomatoes a day you are less likely to get sunburnt and you will keep a lovely complexion well into old age, but he hadn't tested this yet.

All of this seemed a bit far-fetched to me but then so did fly tipping racing greyhounds until I found out different.

Colin was kind, he warned me about the striped Bengal cat, which looked very much like a small monochrome tiger and stood guard at the bottom of the hall stairs. Colin went on to say that the cat had been created by mating an Asian leopard with a domestic tom and was bought for the princely sum of £1,500 from Harrods. I was amazed that such an animal existed since many of the couplings must end up with the domestic tom inside the Asian leopard's stomach.

The Bengal called me over 'My captors continue to taunt me with bizarre little dangling things. They dine lavishly on fresh meat while I am fed on some sort of dry nugget. Although I make my contempt for the dry rations perfectly clear, I never the less eat something to keep up my strength. The only thing that keeps me going is my dream of escape. In my effort to disgust them I vomit on the carpet. Today I decapitated a mouse and dropped its headless body at their feet. I had hoped this would strike fear into their hearts, since it clearly demonstrates what I am capable of. However, they merely made condescending remarks about 'what a good little hunter' I am. They are most definitely, totally inhuman if you ask me'.

After listening at length to the Bengal, I decided the money could have been better spent.

That evening I was treated to a wash and blow dry by her orangeness, followed by an immense dinner of cottage pie for six persons topped with four fried eggs. Colin and I would polish this off before she had a chance to make a dent in own soup and salad.

I discovered from Colin that my current owner is an actress called Katie, who is very pretty and has a ravishing smile. Her mother is a concert pianist and she's the daughter of well-known M.P. We're talking good genes here. And you can see them all in her lovely cheekbones. It would be easy to fall in love with Katie.

She positioned a sumptuous duvet at the foot of her bed and gave me a hand knitted Elvis toy. I decided not to form an emotional attachment to either Katie or hand knitted Elvis because I was soon to be taxied back to the re-homing centre courtesy of the R.S.P.C.A. 'Night-night Vincent' murmured her orangeness sleepily. Firstly, that is not my name and secondly, apart from the ear thing I do not resemble anybody Dutch and ginger. Thirdly, I can't paint.

At breakfast I fell into the habit of chatting with some of the long-term guests, almost all of them actors or theatre people. They lead a charmed studenty existence of Bohemian house-sharing and irresponsible fun with Katie. A favourite was Eric, enormously bulky but very kindly and cheerful, despite the habitually tired bloodhound droop of his eyes. He was looking to play a lawyer in a really good legal series but in the meantime he was a film extra, clanking around in medieval armour in some television commercial that was being shot in the grounds of Katie's house.

The dancing had been, to my untutored non-specialist eye, spectacular, but Katie scribbled savagely in her notebook every time a leg kicked or a body twirled. She was in charge of choreography and if it went badly the whole production would fold; the producer would lose his money and the cast would all be fired. Humiliation all round.

Then a friend of a friend of a friend had heard from the production team that the commercial was good. It was more than good. It was a rave. I stared up at Katie and nuzzled her hand. 'Masterly,' I said. 'If I had a hat, I'd take it off to you.'

A lot of people get quite conscious of their appearance because they're on T.V. but not Katie. She can barely even be bothered to wash her face.

Life with Katie continued its jolly round. When she went off to work, she would switch on the TV in the sitting room 'for company'. On these days, myself, Colin, the Bengal and a few of the neighbouring dogs would get together for an afternoon of games and nibbles. If the weather was good we would play a game in the bit of garden nearest the street where we had to look for a face that would make us leave a house party. Someone so debased or villainous looking that the minute they walked in you'd have to leap out the bathroom window and scuttle down the drainpipe.

Another game we played required us to name the major works of literature we had read. The wriggles of shame at the depths of our ignorance were mortifying. It is something of a relief to know that I was not alone in finding all books unreadable. We also played spin the bottle, hide and seek and charades, a game in which I excelled.

It had nothing to do with my acting, but sprang from a maddening need to show off and be admired.

Katie was funny, very funny. She was also extreme with her fashion sense wearing nothing much more than something that resembled a 1940's night dress and a pair of ill-matched Wellington boots most days...but ditzy or air-headed she is not: she is one of the most intelligent people I have ever met.

It is tempting to be jealous of someone who had so many gifts lavished on them at birth but she has an abundance of kindness and sweetness that makes envy or resentment difficult. She was also very generous with her money, but she never used it to show off. Not once did she make me feel embarrassed or overwhelmed by it. Her kindness was as much in the manner of her generosity and the latter kept me in enviable luxury. Katie's mother often sent large hampers from posh food halls in London, cases of wine, pate, truffles and boxes of exquisite dog biscuits for me and quantities of cashmere socks for her beloved son Rupert.

Breakfast was again delicious but I started to think about Flavia. I am not by nature a pessimist but I did wonder if the door had closed on my previous life with her. So I said to myself, home is not where you live; it's where your owner lives and you're happy. But then a thought crept in saying that within a year of staying with Katie I would become a fatty like the real Elvis and consequently explode. Don't get me wrong, I wasn't unhappy here but it was a bit like being on a lavish holiday. Flavia was truly home for me.

I had a little more time on my hands these days so I took myself down to the pool in Katie's garden and taught myself to swim. None of your fancy lessons either; with sheer will-power I had developed my own powerful idiosyncratic style. It had the added benefit of encouraging people in the pool to avoid me. Learning to swim did nothing to improve my fitness.

The following day it was 47 degrees and drizzling. Knitted Elvis had lost an eye.

Crisis of Confidence

Katie decided that before the inevitable R.S.P.C.A collection she would take some photos and, with a little fiddle of her computer program and some dorky wizardry, up on the screen came the most handsome picture of a hound with just one back-lit ear that was me. However, the days passed and pretty soon she was giving me a massive comedy nose, bunny ears and posting mobile phone footage of me dressed in a silver suit and 'dancing' on YouTube. Rupert, who had the good looks of a floppy haired boy band singer and the habits of an ill-trained but affectionate puppy, had forgotten to phone the R.S.P.C.A. but instead had gone skiing with friends, I realised with quite a heavy heart that I might not see Flavia again.

Katie had lots of friends in London who she would drive up to see for the weekends, taking Rupert, Colin and me with her. On one such car journey Katie said 'Why don't we play a game of some kind to beguile the hours?' They thought for a while then Rupert piped up 'I know. We each have to think of the person whose underpants we would least like on our head.'

'Vincent's', said Katie without a moment's hesitation.

'Ooh, that's not fair' said Rupert laughing, 'you've won already'.

We travelled onwards from London to Manchester which was my first close-up encounter with a television studio and the home of famous soap in which Katie was auditioning for a part, with me playing an 'extra'.

The corridors were lined with photographs of actors and film stars. We were shown down a passageway to a large dressing room where Katie was asked to wait and I was told to 'stay'. We nibbled at crisps and biscuits and grew steadily more nervous. A crew member lead me out to the stage and spent some time positioning me and telling me where and when to move and yelling for silence. My role in this scene, along with everyone else's was to run around and make noise. The camera angles managed to disguise the fact that I had only one ear and numerous grey whiskers but no matter how soulful and sweet I try to appear, my features always arrange themselves into an expression of a warthog. Katie got the part but I didn't. I have rarely been so devastated or felt so cheated. It hurts even now to think that I ran and jumped around the stage like a demented can-can girl, yet lost out to an impish and darkly handsome Border terrier called Pickles.

Maybe Pickles was genuinely more talented than me, or maybe it was the fact that I looked like I'd been dragged off the bottom of a riverbed.

I started to get depressed. Both Colin and the Bengal were bored with me bleating on about how I was incapable of being loved and how I felt unwanted all the time. 'It isn't dignified', said Colin 'it isn't interesting and it isn't attractive' said the Bengal. It was at this low point in my life that Katie took me along to the funeral of her great aunt Alice in Brighton. This was my first-ever trip to Brighton; I was excited about going to a place that had one of the most singularly English pleasures: a walk along the pier. I had to keep hugging myself.

Nowhere else in the world has quite embraced this piece of nineteenth century whimsy. Walk out over the waters! Feel the small thrill of being on dry land and yet! And Yet! Sort of…not! You can see the waters churn through the gaps in the boards! A watery grave could be only moments away! In the meantime, have some candyfloss and listen to the gulls.

The pier extended further and further into the ocean, in some sort of King Canute-style effort to extend man's dominion, and then sell fish and chips there.

Brighton is artistic, bohemian and gay, with boutique hotels and lanes filled with colourful shops selling antiques and the like. Home to the Brighton Pavilion, one of the most exuberantly bizarre buildings I had ever seen, although I wasn't allowed inside but had to settle for the surrounding gardens.

You know that feeling you get during a beautiful romantic island holiday, the feeling that you could stay there all your life. Well, that's what Brighton was like for me, such a fun place to visit. However, you can have too much fun. The funeral of great aunt Alice loomed.

I understood there was to be a buffet of some substance and a few songs sung, including 'Abide With Me' which happened to be one of my favourites. It all sounded a rather jolly affair. I overheard Rupert say great aunt Alice was being mourned as one of the most individual, talented women of her time. The funeral director had been instructed to say a few words about Alice's long career in the theatre.

This was all very interesting to me as I had only met great aunt Alice once and I was totally touched that someone usually so indifferent about the need for pets should invite me to her funeral. I felt honoured and was looking forward to seeing her again.

My expression on the day revealed the unpardonable depths of my ignorance about the whole sad affair. But it got worse.

Katie hadn't read the dress code instructions properly on the funeral invitation. **Sombre**, whilst only being two letters away from **sombrero,** is a world apart in tone.

It was days like these that were able to cast a golden ray of sunshine into my otherwise dull and unremarkable existence.

Katie loved me. She would stroke my big furry chops as she gazed into my soulful brown eyes and she didn't seem to mind the gentle farting noises as I lay by the fire. What I liked most was the evenings sitting in a gormless stupor in front of the television, with a cup of tea and biscuits. This was much better than I was expecting. We'd be mates forever.

I'd heard someone at the re-homing centre once say that 'most dogs need the security of a proper routine with one owner, and without this they become stressed and unhappy'. They were wrong. I wasn't losing sleep or indeed my fur. This dog loves whoever happens to feed him. However, I did wish my life would go backwards to Flavia, her chintz and patterned carpets, floral wallpaper, antimacassars and the bumper pack of dog food that came with it all.

I felt as though I was just marking time with Katie, doing nothing in particular and that I would shuffle off this mortal coil never to see Flavia and her William Morris wallpaper again. These thoughts caused me to sweat. Then, for no reason that anyone can explain to me, a miracle happened. The doorbell rang. I picked up knitted Elvis and ran to open the door as usual, knowing full well that I don't have opposable thumbs and therefore could do no such thing. There stood Flavia, in an ethnic headscarf, wearing sunglasses. I was beside myself with happiness. It turned out that Katie had continued her trawl through the internet lost dog-searching sites to find my true owner. She had emailed the re-homing centre and posted photos of me on Facebook. This was not a thing a dog could grasp.

How perfect is my life. I want to weep when I look back. I got back to Flavia's still shaken by my good fortune. I was the luckiest dog I knew. I came as close to exultation as a dog can.

I have no idea where Katie is now. How did this happen? Presumably when I said good-bye for the last time ever, I really did believe I'd be seeing her again. It wasn't like we'd had an argument and fallen out. I just went home with Flavia and knitted Elvis and never saw Katie again.

Happy Endings

Back in this excellently eccentric house and some weeks later, a media world friend of Flavia's came to visit. A forbiddingly impressive figure of a man called Peter, who was playing this rather defeated father and husband who's going through a divorce. He was possibly the most nicest man in the world. I liked the look of him and his style and you could imagine him climbing under the dinner table and tying someone's shoelaces together. And yes, I could imagine him drunk, easily.

Peter drove a Bentley, sported an old public school tie and had looks that could melt a woman's face. He was married to a tweedy horsey woman who worked at the local Pony Club where she bellowed encouragement to their talentless daughter. Peter had a line in designer crumpled linen suits and a ripely old fashioned 'dear old boy' manner, yet he is the same age as Flavia. He and his third wife were getting divorced and arguing about who got custody of the family dog.

Peter arrived and flung himself on our excellent sofa, pushing me up one end. 'So, old girl what have you been up to since we last met?'

'You remember when we did the panto at University?'

'Er… remind me.'

Flavia flung an impatient cushion at his head. 'You know perfectly well, we did *Aladdin* and you were the Emperor of China and I wrote the script, well I've started writing again.'

'Ah yes, I remember. It was a disaster. A complete disaster. Not a smile, not a titter, nothing. They *hated* us.'

Silence.

'Drink?' asked Flavia.

Peter raised himself off the sofa so I rolled onto my back and stretched out again. He proceeded to pace up and down the sitting room consuming gin and tonic after gin and tonic, becoming more and more hysterical about the absurdity of his marital situation. His and Flavia's pacing routes would converge, and every so often they bumped into one another, 'I don't want to become one of those divorced men who are beaten down by the crushing weight of life, children and alimony' moaned Peter, 'It's true that money and fame do not bring happiness. I'm a well-respected television producer, leading an enviable life, a privileged life but I'm as miserable most days as anybody else', which caused them to burst into fits of manic laughter. The smallest thing would set them off like teenagers.

Peter was a gloriously witty man and he could make Flavia laugh about anything including his response to why she was still single.

'Don't worry Flavia. One day you'll meet a man who'll love you for what you are. Forty.' It really made her laugh.

It turned out that Peter was an old flame of Flavia's and they had hooked up again at some university reunion dinner. To everyone else Peter was just a successful middle-aged man, but to Flavia he was much more than that.

She knew exactly why she had got involved again, but equally she knew the relationship could never last.

Peter later left Flavia to go to his bedroom in a cloud of kisses and extravagant gratitude.

My body clock said it was time for supper but Flavia had disappeared upstairs. And so with heavy heart and even emptier stomach I finished off the cheese biscuits on the lounge table, licked the plate and trudged back to my bed in the kitchen where I fell asleep with knitted Elvis.

The following weekend we were invited by Peter to attend a show in Covent Garden and as we made our way on foot from the stage door to the first-night party, paparazzi closed in on Peter like wasps at a picnic. "This way, Sir Peter.' Flash. 'Sir Peter, Sir Peter!' Flash, pop, flash. Every now and then he would bat them away with a wave of his arm. They would shrink back, mass and swarm again. This continued for the length of our walk.

Flavia's name was beginning to mean a little more in the media world, but there was still no danger of photographers shouting it out on the red carpet. Once or twice though we would be stopped in the street.

'You're that... that woman...'. 'I know I look like her, but I'm not,' she tried saying once or twice. Sunglasses, pulled down beanies and muffled-up scarves make no difference. She might as well be carrying a sign saying that Peter is currently staying with her.

Flavia's publisher friend phoned to say 'Darling, you must finish the book you're writing, you'll get at least a million out of it, no question.' Knowing Peter was beginning to bear fruit.

The following week Flavia was involved in doing a show at the village hall for a homeless charity, it was packed out. She was nervous.

There was a lot of home-made cider about that night and Flavia managed to drink quite a lot of it.

'Is Flavia going to sing during the interval?' asked one of the W.I. members. 'I really think the crowd would like to hear her sing', a proposition which Flavia took strangely seriously. I peeped though the curtain to see her at the edge of the stage, swaying gently as she sang about what would appear to have been an improvised song about a lost love. Then she fell over.

The W,I, member came backstage afterwards looking shell-shocked. 'I think we should have maybe had the raffle during the interval, instead of at the end' she said.

Brilliant. That was clearly what had gone wrong with the evening, everyone agreed.

Shortly afterwards, Peter decided to make another appearance at Flavia's. It was a real relief to me as he clearly made her happy and when he was around she baked cakes. 'That cake is for the grown-ups,' she said. I lurked in the background while she topped up my biscuit bowl. I know there's cake out there so it's hard to eat dog biscuit. I just gave the cake a huge lick as I passed by. I love icing.

Just as I was about to go outside in a fit of boredom, I yawned and breathed in the most enormous moth. I could hear the doorbell ringing whilst I was trying to vomit up a living creature that was flying around my tonsils. It was horrendous. I got as far as the doormat and then puked something that looked like a cross between a bat and a tumour.

The door opened and Flavia beamed. Peter stepped carefully over the doormat and greeted me with 'What the hell?'

Peter liked me very much and spoke to me like he would a child. He said 'One ear is good Jack. Van Gogh pulled that off well and so do you. It makes you look more sinister and interesting.' He'd even trained me to fetch knitted Elvis. In other words he had tried to make me human. But this is futile because I am not human. I know this because when I stayed at his London flat and ended up eating some left over caviar,

I had no concept of Pakistani handmade rugs and consequently emptied the contents of my stomach on his hand-knotted silk Bukhara carpet.

He argued with Flavia about who should clear it up. There was a row and Peter won and now Flavia is not speaking to him.

'Now then Jack, goodnight and you're to behave. Understand?' Peter switched off the light and went up to bed magnificently clad in in blue silk pyjamas,

'Night then, Peter.'

I strained my ears and heard whispering and then Flavia's bed creaking. Then silence.

I was woken by the sound of a lavatory flushing. My duvet was on top of me and the sun was shining through a gap in the curtains. I pulled knitted Elvis towards me and licked him.

I did not know it but this was to mark the beginning of a new act of my life. The tragedy and farce of that drama are the material for another book.

3349858R00032

Printed in Great Britain
by Amazon.co.uk, Ltd.,
Marston Gate.